Fear Nots
For Everyday!

©2009 by Patty Harris
ISBN 978-1-931314-12-1
All rights reserved. No part of this book may be reproduced in any manner whatsoever without the written permission of the Author and Publisher. All scripture references are from the King James Version of the Holy Bible. Published by Olive Press Publishing.

CONTENTS

The Fear of the Lord..3
The Blessings of Fearing God...4
Faith in God..6
I Was Afraid...7
Perverted Faith is Negative Fear.......................................10
Developing the Fear of the Lord.......................................14
Week One - Stand Still and See..18
Week Two - Focus - Focus - Focus..................................36
Week Three - Trust God's Presence..................................54
Week Four - God Will Save..71

The Fear of the Lord

We were created in the image of God. When God created us, He also created our emotions. The emotion of fear that God put within us is called the fear of the Lord and is rooted in faith in God.

The fear of the Lord is the holy and proper spiritual attitude that all believers should have. It is also called Godly fear. The fear of the Lord is the reverential attitude toward God that is born of deep respect for and awe of God. The fear of the Lord is within us and develops through faith and trust in God. It also includes an attitude of not wanting to displease God. When we walk in the fear of the Lord we are careful of what we say and do.

When God created Adam, he walked in the fear of the Lord. Adam walked in complete faith. He totally believed and trusted God. This is the only way Adam and Eve knew to live. They walked in their God given authority and power. The animals and everything created was in subjection to Adam and to Eve.

Although the fear of the Lord does include a fear of God's power and judgment, simply being afraid of God's judgment is not enough to protect our soul from destruction. This "fear of the Lord" should lead us to repentance when we sin. God put fear within us to protect our soul and our body from destruction. He also put within us a natural fear to ensure our safety. This natural fear is what prompts us to get away from a snarling dog or a hissing snake, prompts us to automatically hold up our arms to avoid being hit by something, and causes us to blink our eyes to avoid dust from getting in.

When we fear God, we do not cringe or cower before Him as someone before a cruel dictator. This is not how God wants us to view Him. God desires only the best for and toward us. God tells us in Jeremiah 29: 11 - *For I know the thoughts that I think toward you, saith the LORD, thoughts of peace, and not of evil, to give you an expected end.*

The Blessings of Fearing God

The following verses of scripture give positive aspects and even the blessings of fearing the Lord. The fear of the Lord is strengthened, developed, and matured through a daily relationship with and obedience to the Word of the Lord.

Oh how great is thy goodness, which thou hast laid up for them that fear thee; which thou hast wrought for them that trust in thee before the sons of men! Thou shalt hide them in the secret of thy presence from the pride of man: thou shalt keep them secretly in a pavilion from the strife of tongues. Psalms 31: 19-20

The fear of the Lord prolongeth days: but the years of the wicked shall be shortened. Proverbs 10:27

The fear of the Lord is a fountain of life, to depart from the snares of death. Proverbs 14:27

Praise ye the LORD. Blessed is the man that feareth the LORD, that delighteth greatly in his commandments. His seed shall be mighty upon earth: the generation of the upright shall be blessed. Wealth and riches shall be in his house: and his righteousness endureth for ever. Psalms 112:1-3

Proverbs 14:27
Psalms 112:1-3
Proverbs 10:27
Psalms 31: 19-20

From reading the above scriptures, write some things that are promised to you as you walk in the fear of the Lord.

Notes:

Faith in God

But without faith it is impossible to please him: for he that cometh to God must believe that he is, and that he is a rewarder of them that diligently seek him. Hebrews 11:6
Faith is trust, confidence, and belief in the Word of God. As this scripture tells us if we are to come to God, we must first believe that GOD IS. To have faith in God to deliver you from fear, you must believe that God can and will deliver you from fear and from anything that will harm you.

Sometimes we put our faith in people, our intellect, or our education. God does not want us to put confidence in these things above our faith in Him. God is our Source. When our intellect and education cannot help, God is our Source for wisdom. When people cannot or will not help, God is our Source for strength.

Proverbs 18:10 tells us *The name of the Lord is a strong tower: the righteous runneth into it, and is safe.* We can run into the safety of His name and be safe. You can trust God with your life. He is concerned about your spirit, soul, body, family, finances, and your health. God is even concerned about the things that trouble you or cause you to fear.

Exercise Your Faith in God

Let us therefore fear, lest, a promise being left us of entering into his rest, any of you should seem to come short of it. For unto us was the gospel preached, as well as unto them: but the word preached did not profit them, not being mixed with faith in them that heard it. Hebrews 4:1-2

A key to powerful Christian living is found in verse two; *but the Word preached did not profit them, not being mixed with faith in them that heard it.* The word of God that you receive will only benefit you as you mix it with faith. We are told in Romans 12:2 that God has already given each believer a measure of faith. Therefore, each believer can receive the blessings, promises, deliverance, and answered prayer as you mix His Word with faith.

You must actively pursue what God has promised. Deliverance from fear belongs to every believer. Joy of the Lord is for every believer. Peace of God is for every believer.

"1 was afraid ... "

And the LORD God called unto Adam, and said unto him, Where art thou? 10 And he said. 1 heard thy voice in the garden, and 1 was afraid, because 1 was naked; and 1 hid myself. Genesis 3:9-10

After he had sinned, Adam's first words to God were "I was afraid..." This was not the first time Adam had heard the voice of God in the garden. However, this was the first time that Adam was negatively afraid of the voice of God. God asked Adam, 'Who told you that you were naked?' God knew Adam had been talking to the enemy. Adam was now speaking contrary to God's word. Adam's perception of and relationship with God had now changed. God's word in Adam had now become perverted because it was mixed with the word of the enemy.

The word Adam used for afraid was Yare'. We will use this word many times throughout this study on overcoming negative fears. In the Bible there are two main types of fear described by the word yare'. Let's take a closer look at the meaning of Yare'.

Word Enrichment
YARE'
1. A very positive feeling of awe or reverence for God which may be expressed in piety, formal worship, and daily lifestyle
2. The emotion and intellectual anticipation of harm; what on feels may go wrong for him or her; to be timid, anxious, or afraid.

Adam had only experienced the fear of the Lord. This is a reverence for God which is expressed in one's daily lifestyle.

Adam reverenced God. There had never been any danger for Adam to be concerned about. He only had a reverential fear of the Lord; there was no reason for Adam and Eve to have emotional anticipation of harm or to be anxious for anything. They didn't even know how to die. They only knew how to live.

Living in the continual presence of God was all God had for Adam, Eve, and every believer. Disobedience brings about a change in one's character and life. Sin always does this. When Adam listened to and believed the lie of the enemy, he was bowing his will to the enemy. By doing this, Adam put into motion the law of sin and death which is the perverted law of the Spirit of life in Christ. Everything in the life of Adam and Eve changed when they began to believe the lie of the enemy.

Adam had separated himself from God and therefore was separated from Life! Adam began to die spiritually first, then physically. This is the same process we undergo when we walk in disobedience and separate ourselves from God's Word. Faith and negative fear are closely related and work the same because they are spiritual laws however, they have different results.

Notes:
___
___
___
___
___
___
___
___
___
___
___
___
___
___
___
___
___

Perverted Faith is Negative Fear

For the law of the Spirit of life in Christ Jesus hath made me free from the law of sin and death. Romans 8:2

God created us for life. Through Jesus Christ we are to have the life of God. The devil seeks to keep us from life in Christ. The enemy of our soul comes to steal, kill, and destroy the believer and all that God has for us. God created everything good. The enemy of our souls who cannot create anything can only take what God has created and established - and pervert it.

To pervert something is *to turn it away from its right or proper course; to bring something to a less excellent state.* This is the what the intentions of the enemy are for every believer – to somehow bring the believer into a less excellent state than God created the believer to be. When God created us in His image, God created us to walk in victory and to triumph in all things. Even after Adam and Eve sinned, God sent forth His only begotten Son, Jesus Christ to die and rise with victory from the grave and He gave victory to us. So, we still have victory over the enemy.

The enemy doesn't like that we have God-given power and authority over him and his works. If the devil can get us to think his thoughts, he can get us to act in his ways. This will cause our walk and lifestyle in Christ to become perverted.

Our life will be turned away from the right course that God has for us and the enemy will certainly bring our life to a less excellent state than God intended for us. The enemy understands how the laws of God work. Since the enemy has no creative ability, he can only twist or pervert that which God has already created.

Genesis chapters 1-2 let us know that God created everything good. If we are not walking in the light of God's Word, then we will walk in the darkness of the fear of the enemy.

We were created in the image of God so of course we were created good. With complete authority and dominion over the earth, Adam and Eve walked in faith and in the fear of the Lord.

However, when they disobeyed God, they sold out to the enemy and gave him authority in the earth. The enemy did not and cannot put spiritual laws into motion. The only thing he can do is pervert the spiritual laws that God has already established.

We cannot go against the ways and word of God and expect the best. The best for us is to walk in obedience to God's will. Are you walking in obedience to God's Word to you? Take some time to think about this. What was the last instruction God gave to you? Have you been obedient to it? If we are not walking in obedience to the Word of God, we open the door for the enemy to bring in negative fear.

What have you been walking in? Be honest with yourself and with God. You cannot be free from fear until you are honest with your obedience to God.

We can depend on a law to work the same way every time. For example, the law of gravity says "what goes up must come down." This law works the same way all the time for every person.

The Word and ways of God will always overcome whatever the enemy has said and/or done. When we walk in disobedience to God, our lives become distorted and perverted. Our life turns away from the right course that God has designed for us. The right course would be that of walking in faith and the fear of the Lord. However, when we obey the enemy, the life God designed for us becomes misguided. Adam and Eve still had faith, however, it was now perverted. Their faith, which caused them to exercise complete fear of the Lord, had turned to negative fear, which is perverted faith.

Let's look at some of the things the enemy has perverted:

1- FAITH
Fear is perverted Faith

We are to walk in the faith which is the fear of the Lord. Faith is trust, confidence in God. God did not create us to walk in negative fear. Negative fear is not a new law that the enemy created. It is the perverted law of faith. Faith will overcome fear.

The law of sin and death is the twisted or perverted law of the Spirit of life in Christ Jesus. The Spirit of life in Christ will overcome the spirit of death.

2 - LIFE
Death is perverted life

"...1am come that you might have life, and that you might have it more abundantly. " John 10: 10b

Death is perverted Life – The thief cometh not, but for to steal, and to kill, and to destroy ... John 10:10a

3- LOVE
Hatred is perverted love

In this was manifested the love of God toward us, because that God sent his only begotten Son into the world, that we might live through him.

Hatred is perverted Love – The thief cometh not, but for to steal, and to kill, and to destroy ... John 10:Ioa

4 – PEACE
Worry is perverted peace

Peace I leave with you, my peace I give unto you: not as the world giveth, give I unto you. John 14:27

Worry/anxiety is perverted Peace - The thief cometh not, but for to steal, and to kill, and to destroy ... John 10:l0a

5 – PROSPERITY

Poverty is perverted prosperity

Beloved, I wish above all things that thou mayest prosper and be in health, even as thy soul prospereth. 3 John 2

Poverty is perverted Prosperity - The thief cometh not, but for to steal, and to kill, and to destroy. ... John 10:10a

DEVELOPING THE FEAR OF THE LORD!
involves an
ACTIVE FAITH PLAN

Praise ye the Lord. Blessed is the man that feareth the Lord, that delighteth greatly in His commandments. Psalms 112:1

My son, attend to my words; incline thine ear unto my sayings. 2 Let them not depart from thine eyes; keep them in the midst of thine heart. 22 For they are life unto those that find them, and health to all their flesh. 23 Keep thy heart with all diligence; for out of it are the issues of life. Proverbs 4:20-23

I sought the Lord, and he heard me, and delivered me from all my fears. Psalms 34:4

    In Psalms 34:4, David tells how he sought the Lord for his deliverance from fears. In these lessons, you are seeking the Lord for deliverance from fears. Something happened to David as he sought the Lord. God heard David AND God delivered David from all David's fears! God will do the same for everyone who calls on and trusts in Him!

    The word David used for fears in this scripture is *mguwrah*. It means *terror, anxiety from being in a strange place where one is not at home*. The root of this word is *guwr*. This root word means *to turn aside from the road for the purpose of lodging for the night; to dwell as a stranger*.

    As Christians we should be very uncomfortable when we are afraid. We should live as strangers to negative fears. God has created us to live in faith and the fear of the Lord, not in torment and anxiety that the enemy brings to us as a result of perverted faith. Love for God and believing how much God loves us will cast out the fear that causes terror and torment to the believer.

    You must be active in overcoming the fears that hinder your spiritual growth and affect your relationship with God.

    The only way to overcome negative fear is to develop the fear of the Lord. Faith is an action word.

As you develop and strengthen your faith in God, the fear of the Lord will increase. This is done through the Word of God. It is not enough to read the Word. Mix the Word with faith and do something with what you read. Faith without works or activity is dead and useless.

You must activate the Word by believing it and speaking it in every situation, even speaking it to yourself. The enemy will try to put thoughts into your mind. The enemy will try to make you think "you are in new territory, this won't work for you. You can't accomplish this. Don't be stupid you'll fail - again!"

The only way to overcome the thoughts of the enemy is with spoken Words. Thoughts will not get rid of thoughts. You must speak the Word of God and speak it aloud. You must hear yourself speak the Word of God.

The Word must get into your spirit, soul, and your mouth to overcome the enemy. You must be determined to be free. It takes time to be free. God can deliver you miraculously however, you would go back to your old way of thinking. This is why you have to seek the Lord - just as David did.

Seek God! Continually! Daily! Make time for the Word of God! This allows the Holy Spirit to create permanent change in one's thinking and believing so that transformation can occur in one's life! God will answer when you call and speak His Word.

Your faith will be strengthened as you put it to use! God will not do it for you. God has made His strength, power, anointing, and authority available to those who believe in Jesus Christ as God's only begotten Son, and who have accepted Jesus Christ as personal Lord and Savior. If you have done this, you have the life of God dwelling within you. However, the enemy will try to ensnare you with your past and with ignorance of applying the Word of God to your life. The Word works if you work it and speak it! Your fears can be conquered if you apply the Word to your life.

This month long study takes discipline. Before you progress to Book #2, be sure you have mastered the principles in this book. The Active Faith Plan (AFP) is to help you discipline yourself in studying and applying the Word of God to daily life.

You have to be transformed by the renewing of your mind. Thoughts contrary to the Word of God must be eliminated. This takes time and discipline. The Holy Spirit will begin to transform your life from within. Changes will begin to take place in your life as you apply the Word. You will begin to be transformed by the renewing of your mind.

Why the same plan for a month?

Discipline and review! To get rid of thoughts that cause fear, they must be replaced with the Word that builds faith. This does not always happen overnight You are in God's process of renewal and restoration. The enemy will fight, however, you must remain steadfast and faithful to God and to yourself if you want to be free from fear and torment.

God loves you so much - He sent His Son to set you free from the enemy! God has done all that He can do - the rest is up to you. God is on your side.

Write the fears that you have. Beside each one write a prayer thanking God for delivering you from it. There will be many scriptures to review so you may want to write a scripture beside the fear also as a sign of God's promise to you.

The closer our relationship and walk with God, the stronger will be our caution or fear that we are displeasing God. God intended for fear to keep us from doing wrong, and thereby protect our soul from eternal destruction.

God intended for fear to keep us close to Him, however, when the enemy twists the God-given emotion of fear, he uses twisted fear against us to keep us from God and all that is good for us.

Why a daily confession?

We believe what we hear ourselves say. To confess means to say the same as another; to agree. You must agree with what God has said and speak it. Think about what you've been thinking about. Are you saying things that are contrary to the Word of God? If so, that means the enemy has you speaking perversion. If the enemy has you speaking it, he will have you living it. Confess and align your words with what God says.

Each week there is a different topic to read and think through.

Week One - Stand Still!
Week Two - Focus!
Week Three - Trust God's Presence!
Week Four - God will Save!

Each day you will have an Active Faith Plan to read and follow:

1 - **Monday** - Submit yourself to God's Word
2 - **Tuesday** - Meditate the Word of God
3 - **Wednesday** - Believe and Speak the Word of God
4 - **Thursday** - Be a doer of the Word of God
5 - **Friday** - Trust God's Faithfulness to God's Word

Saturdays and Sundays are for personal review of what you've read that week or a time to cath up on what you missed.

The **Word Enrichment** sections give definitions of some of the words in Hebrew (OT) and Greek (NT). This is to help clarify the meaning and understanding of scriptures.

Week One
Stand Still and See
Exodus 14:13-14

And Moses said unto the people, Fear ye not, stand still, and see the salvation of the LORD, which he will show to you t day, for the Egyptians whom ye have seen to day, ye shall see them again no more for ever. (14) The LORD shall fight for you, and ye shall hold your peace.

Word Enrichment

Stand still - (yasab); to remain; to place anything so as to stay; to speak truth; to be firm

Salvation - (Jeshua); help, deliverance, victory. The source of this salvation, help, and deliverance comes from outside the situation of oppression. It gives the idea of being comfortable and having no problems.

Show - (awsaw); to make, create; build, prepare. This word is use to describe God's creative activity.

As the Israelites were crossing the Red Sea they saw the Egyptians in the distance speeding after them. They became terribly frightened and cried out to God for help. While they cried to God, they complained to Moses and blamed him for bringing them into the wilderness to die.

With the Red Sea before them and the enemy following after them what would they do? Who knew how to swim? Could they even swim that far? They were unarmed. How could they fight against the mighty armies of Pharaoh? What would their punishment be if the enemy overtook them out here in the wilderness? Their situation seemed helpless and hopeless.

They wanted to be free from bondage, however, when things became difficult they began to murmur and complain. They even wished to return to their bondage and slavery in Egypt. They were comfortable in bondage because they knew what to expect.

There are times when like the Israelites, we are on the road to freedom and here comes the enemy. Double mindedness is a tactic the enemy uses to cause us to doubt God's word. When we begin to doubt the Word of God we will vacillate. Should I go back?

One minute we believe God's Word is true. The next minute, usually when things get rough, we don't know if God will fulfill His promise. James 1:8 tells us that *a double-minded person will not receive from God.* The enemy knows this and he uses it against us to hinder us from receiving from God. Double mindedness has its roots in fear.

It was difficult for the children of Israel to see how God would deliver them out of this situation. They were delivered out of Egypt, now here are their task masters following close behind them ready to overtake them. It usually seems that as you leave one situation thinking and believing you are on the right road, you run right into another difficult situation.

When our backs are against the wall it is difficult to see how God will bring us safely through. This causes our hearts to negatively fear instead of walking in the fear of the Lord which is faith. The enemy distorts our view. Don't be discouraged or dismayed - God will fight for you.

Just as the Israelites did, we call on God, yet still murmur and complain about the situation we are in. Don't pray the situation or the problem - pray the answer which is found in the Word of the Lord.

We don't have to know how God will heal or deliver. We simply have to exercise active faith in God's promises to help, heal, and deliver. God does not want us to be tormented with perverted fear. God will supply our every need and God will usually do it creatively. God doesn't deliver according to what we can see. God's creativity is far beyond anything we can think of.

We must take the limits off God. When we ask God for help, we must trust Him. We must trust God in confidence not with complaining. As we trust God, fear and the torments that it brings will flee from us and we will see and experience His salvation in the situations we encounter.

The children of Israel were given three exhortations: (1) Fear Not (2) Stand still, and (3) See.

They were experiencing the negative side of yare' which is the emotion and intellectual anticipation of harm; what one feels may go wrong for him or her; to be timid, anxious, or afraid. God did not want them to put their confidence here.

God simply told them 'Don't fear.' God knew in the natural their situation looked hopeless. We must remember when God says 'Fear not' it is usually because in the natural there is a reason to fear.

The second exhortation was to 'stand still.' Once their minds were fixed on the Lord that is the place where their thoughts were to stay. One of the Hebrew meanings of 'stand still' is 'to place anything so as to stay. They were to put their faith and confidence in what God
said and remain there. They were to keep their minds on the Word
of the Lord. This is the only thing that would give them constant
stability during such a difficult situation.

We must discipline our thoughts to 'stand still.' Thoughts can and will run wild if will allow them too. Many times we will become anxious or worried because our thoughts are scattered.

We look at the situation and think "..What if this doesn't work out?" or "I don't see any way through this. " Our thoughts must remain firm on what God has said! This is what will give us stability as well as peace of mind and soul.

The third exhortation was to simply' see.' If they put their faith in God, remained steadfast in the Word of God, God would fight their enemies. They would be able to see the salvation of the Lord. The deliverance that God worked for them, God worked independently of human help and interference.

Monday: Stand Still and See
"SUBMIT YOURSELF TO GOD"

Submit yourselves therefore to God. Resist the devil, and he will flee from you. James 4:7

Word Enrichment

Submit - to yield to; surrender; to obey; to defer to another's opinion or decision; to agree. The opposite of submit is to fight.

Submit - (hupotasso); to place in an orderly fashion under. Hupa tasso is made up of two words: hupo, which means under. Hupo implies placement i.e., beneath, or to place under.

The other word is tasso. Tasso means to place, set in order or in its proper category. Tasso has inherent in its meaning order, categoriza tion, and classification.

Resist - (anthistemi); to oppose; to act or make efforts in opposition to; to do something that prevents or inhibits some effect from taking place.

Flee - to run away from danger or from pursuers; to run from a place or person; to take flight.

We must agree with the Word of God and walk in obedience to it. This is how we place ourselves under the authority of God's Word. As we place our will and our words in order under God's Word, the rest of our life will begin to line up with the blessings that God has for us. Our life will begin to have more order as we place it under God's authority.

To overcome negative fears one must first submit to God and God's Word. Only after you have done that will you be able to resist the enemy. In submitting to God, you are resisting the enemy. Concentrate on submitting to God not on resisting the enemy. Resistance is a process. For example, when you have a wooden deck put in your yard it must be treated with a weather resistant to prevent corrosion from the rain, snow and inclement weather. As you continually submit to God with complete obedience, the Word of God in you will resist the enemy and prevent the corrosion of corrupt thinking to overtake your life.

Stand still! Remain firm in the Word by submitting your thoughts and conduct to God. You will see the enemy flee. The enemy will run away from us, not because of us, but because of Christ in us.

Is there an area where you have been afraid to submit your thinking to the Word of God? Choose today to submit your thinking to the word of God. For example, if you think negatively about someone, ask God to help them and to bless them; if you fear you will not have enough money (after you have tithed) thank God for supplying all your needs according to His riches in glory! If you fear your household will not be saved, thank God for saving you and for being faithful that He would save your entire household.

-Is there an area in your life where you have not submitted your behavior to the Word of God? Today, choose three behaviors that you know are contrary to God's Word and submit them to God.

This means you will behave the opposite of how you've been behaving. For example, if you have not forgiven someone, choose to forgive them. If you always get to work late, get to work on time and leave on time. Get the idea? If you've been undisciplined with your time alone with God - make time to be with God.

ACTIVE FAITH PRAYER:

Lord Jesus, I yield myself to You: spirit, soul, and body. Be Lord and Savior of my entire life. Lord, plead my cause with them that strive with me: fight against them that fight against me. Take hold of shield and buckler, and stand up for my help. In Jesus name, amen.

ACTIVE FAITH CONFESSION:
I will fear not, stand still, and see the salvation of the Lord. I will trust in the Lord and obey His Word.

Notes:

Tuesday: Stand Still and See
"MEDITATE THE WORD"

This book of the law shall not depart out of thy mouth; but thou shalt meditate therein day and night. that thou mayest observe to do according to all that is written therein: for then thou shalt make thy way prosperous, and then thou shalt have good success. Joshua 1:8

Word Enrichment

Meditate - (hagah); to mutter to oneself, to whisper, to speak. It is possible that the Scriptures were read audibly during the process of meditation. Hagah also describes the low moaning sound of a dove.

Many people think that meditation is a difficult discipline. If you know how to worry, then you know how to meditate. Worry is simply negative meditation. In meditation, you review something over and over again either in your mind or aloud. Instead of reviewing a problem, rehearse in your mind the answer which is found in the Word of God.

Meditation allows us to quiet our spirit and soul from the things that daily clamor for our attention. We become quiet within. There is no frenzied and hurried activity during meditation! Simply, quietly, and plainly be in the presence of God knowing that God is with you. Meditating on a verse or passage of scripture allows us to marinate in the Word and gives the Word opportunity to saturate throughout our inner being. In meditation we marinate and saturate the Word!!!

Basics of meditating: Take five minutes. Sit, stand, or lie down in a relaxed position in a quiet place where you cannot be disturbed. Inhale deep breaths and count as you exhale. Counting your breath helps to practice the ability of thinking of one thing at a time. Simply breathe and count. If other thoughts come, realize you are straying from your instructions and gently bring yourself to counting again. Do this for three to five minutes twice a day. The third time you do this during the day, review a meditation scripture or just quietly give thanks to God.

You can also spend time in silence before Him. An important aspect of meditation is follow-through. Decide the time and place you will spend meditating, not the time you'd like to spend meditating. Growth and change take time. Be determined to stick with it. Be faithful. The benefits of meditating are tremendous. The more you dwell on the Word of God, the more it will season your soul and spirit. Be faithful. You will see and experience the benefits of meditation.

Write and Meditate the following scripture
throughout the day:
Exodus 14:13-14

_____
_____
_____
_____
_____
_____
_____
_____
_____
_____
_____
_____
_____
_____
_____
_____
_____
_____
_____
_____
_____
_____

ACTIVE FAITH PRAYER:

Thank You Jesus for saving me. You have carried me through many difficult situations. You have forgiven all my sins and iniquities. Thank You Jesus!!! Help me to grow in the grace and knowledge of You, my Savior, and my Lord. As I learn to meditate, help me to fear not, to stand still that I may see Your salvation on my behalf. In Jesus name. Amen.

ACTIVE FAITH CONFESSION:

I will meditate the Word of God. It shall cause me to be prosperous and have good success.

Notes:

Wednesday: Stand Still and See
"BELIEVE AND SPEAK THE WORD OF GOD"

That if thou shalt confess with thy mouth the Lord Jesus, and shalt believe in thine heart that God hath raised him from the dead, thou shalt be saved. For with the heart man believeth unto righteousness; and with the mouth confession is made unto salvation. Romans 10:9-10

Word Enrichment

Confess - (homologeo); to say the same as; to speak the same with or consent to the desire of another; to covenant; to give thanks; acknowledge; speak in harmony with the truth.

Salvation - (soteria); deliverance; preservation; safety; Soteria is the spiritual and eternal salvation granted by God to those who believe in Jesus Christ. Soteria is also used of material and temporal deliverance from danger, suffering, sickness, etc.

We must begin to confess what the Word of God says. What have you been saying? Have you been speaking fear filled words of the enemy or have you been speaking the faith filled Word of God? In Matthew 4 when Jesus was tempted of the devil, He who is the Word made flesh spoke the Word to the enemy. We must do the same.

To be saved from the destruction and torments of fear, you must begin to believe and say what God has said to you and about you. Do not allow the enemy to pervert your thinking and your words any longer. Jesus tells us in John 6:63 that the words He speaks are Spirit and life. We are also told in Proverbs 18:21 that death and life are in the power of the tongue. Words do something. Words create! We believe that Jesus came to give us life more abundantly and that Jesus speaks words that are spirit and life.

SPEAK WHAT JESUS SPEAKS!!! The Word of God will change the way you think and view your life, your circumstances and your situations.

Amos 3:3 asks 'Can two walk together, except they be agreed?' You cannot walk with God and receive all that God has for you until you walk in agreement with God's Word. If you don't agree with God you will agree with the enemy who is totally against you and perverts what God has said. God is always for your good.

BELIEVE AND AGREE WITH GOD!!!

What has caused my heart to be fearful? Anxious?
~ What am I saying about it?
~Am I speaking faith or fear?

Today choose a situation in your life that has caused you to be fearful. Believe, speak, and spend time meditating Isaiah 41: 10 aloud to yourself about this situation.

Isaiah 41:10

_____
_____
_____
_____
_____
_____
_____
_____
_____
_____
_____
_____
_____
_____

ACTIVE FAITH PRAYER:

O Lord, when my heart is overwhelmed; lead me to that Rock that is higher than I. Thank You for being a shelter for me and a strong tower from the enemy of fear. Thank You, Lord for saving me from the plans of the enemy and delivering me from fear. In Jesus name Amen.

ACTIVE FAITH CONFESSION:

I will trust in the Lord forever; for in the Lord Jehovah is everlasting strength (Isaiah 26:4) The LORD is my light and my salvation; whom shall I fear? The LORD is the strength of my life; of whom shall I be afraid? When the wicked, even mine enemies and my foes, came upon me to eat up my flesh, they stumbled and fell. Though an host should encamp against me, my heart shall not fear: though war should rise against me, in this will I be confident (Psalms 27:1-3) that no weapon that is formed against me shall prosper; and every tongue that shall rise against me in judgment I shalt condemn. This is the heritage of the servants of the LORD, and their righteousness is of me, saith the LORD. (Isaiah 54:17).

Thursday: Stand Still and See
"BE A DOER OF THE WORD"
But be ye doers of the word, and not hearers only, deceiving your own selves. James 1:22

Word Enrichment

Doer - (poietes); A performer; one who performs from a script. Poietes/doer is one who reads a script and then acts out what the script says.

   Many times we read the Word of God even hear it taught, however, we fail to do the Word of God. We must put the Word of God into action in our life. Just as a performer reads a script and acts out what the script says, this is what we must do with the Word. Act as if the Word of God is true. The children of Israel were told to do two things and they would see and experience the salvation of God in the midst of their circumstances. They were told to (1) Stand still and (2) Fear Not! These are actions that we must do also.
   Believe the Word of God. Act on the Word of God. The Word says that you are free - so walk in the freedom Christ Jesus gave to you. Don't listen to the words of the enemy that are against the Word of God. We cannot fulfill the word of God on our own. This is why God gave us His Holy Spirit. As the Holy Spirit leads and guides us into the truth of God's Word, we must walk in obedience.

What has God told you to do?
Have you done it? Has fear hindered you?
What are you going to do about it?

   If God has told you to do something then God will supply the ability and the power for you to do it. You can be a doer of the word without fear because God is on your side!

ACTIVE FAITH PRAYER:

Thank You, Lord for teaching me to be a doer of Your Word. Help me to stand firm in Your word, to fear not those situations in life which are challenging to me. Thank You, God that I will see Your salvation in each situation. In Jesus name, Amen.

ACTIVE FAITH CONFESSION:

I will bless the Lord at all times. His praises shall continually be in my mouth (Psalms 34.) I will love thee, LORD, my strength. The LORD is my rock, and my fortress, and my deliverer; my God, my strength, in whom I will trust; my buckler, and the horn of my salvation, and my high tower. I will call upon the LORD, who is worthy to be praised: so shall I be saved from mine enemies (Psalms 181-3)

Notes:
_____
_____
_____
_____
_____
_____
_____
_____
_____
_____
_____
_____
_____
_____
_____

Friday: Stand Still and See
'TRUST GOD'S FAITHFULNESS"

This I recall to my mind, therefore have I hope. 22 It is of the LORD'S mercies that we are not consumed, because his compassions fail not. 23 They are new every morning: great is thy faithfulness. Lamentations 3:21-23

Word Enrichment

Recall- (shuv); to turn oneself around; to turn to Jehovah; to restore; the basic meaning of shuv is movement back to the point of departure.

Mind - (lev); the heart, middle, or the center of something. Lev is used for the totality of man's inner immaterial nature. These are the deepest and innermost feelings. In the Bible, the entire spectrum of our human emotions is related to and attributed to the heart.

Hope - (yachal); to wait; to expect; to be patient. Yachal is rooted in God

Mercies - (chesed); unfailing love; favor; benevolence; good will; loyalty

Faithfulness - (emunah); firmness; steadiness; trust; honesty

As we read through the beginning of this chapter we see that Jeremiah was rehearsing all the bad things that had happened to him and God's people. Does that sound familiar. We often rehearse things that have gone wrong for us or the things that we have done that were wrong. We blame God, self, or others.

No matter what has happened God is not mad at you! God still loves you and has a wonderful plan for your life. He loves, forgives, saves, heals, and delivers every believer who calls on Him from every destruction. At verse 21, we see Jeremiah coming to the truth that God is still with him.

He had to shuv/recall to his mind. To shuv is to return to the point of departure. Jeremiah had departed from his belief that God is with him.

This departure caused him to review in his mind all the negatives of live. His hope was gone until he returned his thinking to the faithfulness of God, realizing he was still experiencing new mercies of God each day! Even in the midst of rough situations, God's compassions did not fail Jeremiah. God is on your side.

Whatever has happened begin to trust God now as your Salvation, Healer, and Deliverer from fears and torment. God is faithful! In our opening text, God was leading His children along. They were fine until they saw the enemy! After they saw the enemy the children of Israel began to fear which was followed by murmuring and complaining to Moses.

God did not beat them over the head! He gently told them, "Fear not, stand still, and see My salvation." This is what we must remember to do when adverse situations come our way. Don't look at and meditate all the negatives: what has gone wrong and what doesn't look right. Recall to your mind the goodness and mercies of the Lord. This gives stability and hope.

~ What situation are you in that you cannot see God working on your behalf?

Write and Meditate the following scripture today: Lamentations 3:21-23

_____
_____
_____
_____
_____
_____
_____
_____
_____

_____
_____
_____
_____
_____
_____
_____
_____
_____
_____
_____
_____

ACTIVE FAITH PRAYER:

Hear my cry, O God; attend unto my prayer. I praise You for Your faithfulness, Your mercy, and Your grace toward me. Great is Your faithfulness to me and I praise Your name. Lord God, when I can't see Your hand, help me to trust Your heart. Thank You for loving me and caring for me all the days of my life. In Jesus name, Amen.

ACTIVE FAITH CONFESSION:

God is with me. I will not fear. I've been redeemed by the blood of Jesus from the hand of the enemy. The blood of Jesus covers me, angels are encamped around me, underneath me are the everlasting arms of a loving Savior, goodness and mercy are following me. I will not fear. God is with me and I will trust God's faithfulness to me.

Week 2
Focus! Focus! Focus!
II Kings 6:16-17

And he answered, Fear not: for they that be with us are more than they that be with them. And Elisha prayed, and said, LORD, I pray thee, open his eyes, that he may see. And the LORD opened the eyes of the young man; and he saw: and, behold, the mountain was full of horses and chariots of fire round about Elisha.

Word Enrichment

Focus - An adjustment of the focal length in order to produce a clear image; any center of attention, activity, etc.; to fix or settle on one thing; to adjust one's eye or lense to make a clear image.

Open - (paqah); to be observant; be clearsighted

When the enemy surrounded the entire city with hosts, horses, and chariots, Elisha's servant saw them and became disturbed in mind. When we look at and concentrate on the overwhelming forces of the enemy, we become fearful. Being afraid, the young servant of Elisha asked, "What shall we do?" The enemy was mighty and there were many enemies surrounding them.

So often we find ourselves in situations and ask "What shall I do?" Some situations occur in life that would cause us to fear because of overwhelming emotional pressures. It might seem that everywhere you go, the enemy is there to intimidate you and make you think that God is not with you. When it seems that God is not with you, child of God, you can rejoice. Tell yourself God is in and with me by His Spirit and Greater is He that is within me than he that is within the world (I Thess. 4:4). The presence of God is always with, near, and in the believer.

God is within the believer by His Spirit. We see with our natural eyes that which is in the natural realm. We see by faith in our spirit that which is in the spiritual realm. It is crucial to remember that what is seen naturally is not all there is. The spiritual realm is more real than the natural.

The angels of the Lord are encamped around those who fear and trust in the Lord. You are the majority when God is with you. Focusing helps us to get grounded in God's word. We must make the Word of God the center of our attention.

Notes:

Monday: Focus!Focus!Focus!
"SUBMIT YOURSELF TO GOD"

Submit yourselves therefore to God. Resist the devil. and he will flee from you. James 4:7

Word Enrichment

Submit - to yield to; surrender; to obey; to defer to another's opinion or decision; to agree. The opposite of submit is to fight.

Submit - (hupotasso); to place in an orderly fashion under. Hupatasso is made up of two words: hupo, which means under. Hupo implies placement i.e., beneath, or to place under.

The other word is tasso. Tasso means to place, set in order or in its proper category. Tasso has inherent in its meaning order, categorization, and classification.

Resist - (anthistemi); to oppose; to act or make efforts in opposition to; to do something that prevents or inhibits some effect from taking place.

Flee - to run away from danger or from pursuers; to run from a place or person; to take flight.

We must agree with the Word of God and walk in obedience to it. This is how we place ourselves under the authority of God's Word. As we place our will and our words in order under God's Word, the rest of our life will begin to line up with the blessings that God has for us. Our life will begin to have more order as we place it under God's authority.

To overcome negative fears one must first submit to God and God's Word. Only after you have done that will you be able to resist the enemy. In submitting to God, you are resisting the enemy.

Concentrate on submitting to God not on resisting the enemy. Resistance is a process. For example, when you have a wooden deck put in your yard it must be treated with a weather resistant to prevent corrosion from the rain, snow and inclement weather.

As you continually submit to God with complete obedience, the Word of God in you will resist the enemy and prevent the corrosion of corrupt thinking to overtake your life.

Stand still! Remain firm in the Word by submitting your thoughts and conduct to God. You w ill see the enemy flee. The enemy will run away from us, not because of us, but because of Christ in us.

Psalms 34:4 says I sought the LORD, and he heard me, and delivered me from all my fears. This word fears is not the yare' that we've been studying. The word for fear in this verse is *megura*. Megura is *the object of fear*.

The object of fear was the armies of the enemy which the young man could see in the natural. Seeing on the outside disturbed him on the inside. He was robbed of peace. Elisha told him yare. Don't be afraid of what could go wrong. He then prayed for God to open the young man's eyes.

This young man needed spiritual vision of the presence of God. He was focusing on the wrong scene. We must seek the Lord for the answers we need. In seeking God we remain focused on His Word and not the situations that create fear.

Where is your focus?

Are you more confident in the object of fear or of the presence of God?

Do you believe God is with you?

Notes:

_____
_____
_____
_____
_____
_____
_____
_____
_____
_____
_____
_____
_____
_____
_____
_____
_____
_____

ACTIVE FAITH PRAYER:

Help me Lord to stay focused on Your word and trust You to deliver Me from all my fears. In Jesus name, amen.

ACTIVE FAITH CONFESSION:
I will submit myself to the Word of God. I will resist then devil, and he will flee from me.

Tuesday: Focus! Focus! Focus!
"MEDITATE THE WORD"

This book of the law shall not depart out of thy mouth; but thou shalt meditate therein day and night, that thou mayest observe to do according to all that is written therein: for then thou shalt make thy way prosperous, and then thou shalt have good success. Joshua 1:8

Word Enrichment

Meditate - (hagah); to mutter to oneself, to whisper, to speak. It is possible that the Scriptures were read audibly during the process of meditation.

Hagah also describes the low moaning sound of a dove.

Many people think that meditation is a difficult discipline. If you know how to worry, then you know how to meditate. Worry is simply negative meditation. In meditation, you review something over and over again either in your mind or aloud. Instead of reviewing a problem, rehearse in your mind the answer which is found in the Word of God.

Meditation allows us to quiet our spirit and soul from the things that daily clamor for our attention. We become quiet within. There is no frenzied and hurried activity during meditation! Simply, quietly, and plainly be in the presence of God knowing that God is with you. Meditating on a verse or passage of scripture allows us to marinate in the Word and gives the Word opportunity to saturate throughout our inner being. In meditation we marinate and saturate the Word!!!

Basics of meditating: Take five minutes. Sit, stand, or lie down in a relaxed position in a quiet place where you cannot be disturbed. Inhale deep breaths and count as you exhale. Counting your breath helps to practice the ability of thinking of one thing at a time. Simply breathe and count. If other thoughts come, realize you are straying from your instructions and gently bring yourself to counting again. Do this for three to five minutes twice a day.

The third time you do this during the day, review a meditation scripture or just quietly give thanks to God. You can also spend time in silence before Him. An important aspect of meditation is follow-through. Decide the time and place you will spend meditating, not the time you'd like to spend meditating. Growth and change take time. Be determined to stick with it. Be faithful. The benefits of meditating are tremendous. The more you dwell on the Word of God, the more it will season your soul and spirit. Be faithful. You will see and experience the benefits of meditation.

Notes:
_____
_____
_____
_____
_____
_____
_____
_____
_____
_____
_____
_____
_____
_____
_____
_____
_____
_____
_____

ACTIVE FAITH PRAYER:

O Lord, help me to be disciplined and focused in Your Word. Teach me Thy way and lead me. In Jesus' name, Amen.

ACTIVE FAITH CONFESSION:

Thank You Lord for opening my eyes that I may see wondrous things in Your Word.

Write and Meditate Psalms 119:18 today.

_____
_____
_____
_____
_____
_____
_____
_____
_____
_____
_____
_____
_____
_____
_____
_____
_____
_____
_____
_____
_____
_____
_____
_____

Word Enrichment

Open (ghalah); unveil; to be uncovered

Wondrous things (pala); remarkable; to act miraculously; astonishing; extraordinary. Pala is the clear cut exhibition of God' divine and capable care.

Wednesday: Focus! Focus! Focus!
"BELIEVE AND SPEAK THE WORD OF GOD"

That if thou shalt confess with thy mouth the Lord Jesus, and shalt believe in thine heart that God hath raised him from the dead, thou shalt be saved. 10 For with the heart man believeth unto righteousness; and with the mouth confession is made unto salvation. Romans 10:9-10

Word Enrichment

Confess - (homologeo); to say the same as; to speak the same with or consent to the desire of another; to covenant; to give thanks; To acknowedge; to speak in harmony with the truth.

Salvation - (soteria); deliverance; preservation; safety; Soteria is the spiritual and eternal salvation granted by God to those who believe on Jesus Christ.

Soteria is also used of material and temporal deliverance from danger suffering, sickness, etc.

We must begin to confess what the Word of God says. What have you been saying? Have you been speaking fear filled words of the enemy or have you been speaking the faith filled Word of God?

In Matthew 4 when Jesus was tempted of the devil, He who is the Word made flesh spoke the Word to the enemy. We must do the same. To be saved from the destruction and torments of fear, you must begin to believe and say what God has said to you and about you. Do not allow the enemy to pervert your thinking and your words any longer. Jesus tells us in John 6:63 that the words He speaks are spirit and life. We are also told in Proverbs 18:21 that death and life are in the power of the tongue. Words do something. Words create!

We believe that Jesus came to give us life more abundantly and that Jesus speaks words that are spirit and life. SPEAK WHAT JESUS SPEAKS!!! The Word of God will change your life, your circumstances and your situations.

Amos 3:3 asks 'Can two walk together, except they be agreed?' You cannot walk with God and receive all that God has for you until you walk in agreement with God's Word. If you don't agree with God you will agree with the enemy who is totally against you and perverts what God has said. God is always for your good.

If our confidence in God's word is weak, we will not have good spiritual vision. When this happens, we cannot boldly speak victory. Elisha could speak confidently and boldly because he saw clearly. His eyes were opened because his heart had received and believed the word of God.

The young man saw the danger, Elisha saw the protective hand of Almighty God in the midst of the danger. When our focus is rooted in the Sovereignty and power of Almighty God, we won't be easily disturbed and fear the troubles on earth.

BELIEVE AND AGREE WITH GOD!!!
~ What situation is causing my heart to be fearful? Anxious?
~Am I speaking faith or fear?
Today choose a situation in your life that has caused you to be fearful. Believe, speak, and spend time meditating Isaiah 41: 10 aloud to yourself about this situation.

ACTIVE FAITH PRAYER:
Thank You God for helping me to only speak what Your word says to be true about me. In Jesus' name, Amen.

ACTIVE FAITH CONFESSION:
Lord Jesus, I believe in You!

Thursday: Focus! Focus! Focus!
"BE A DOER OF THE WORD"

But be ye doers of the word, and not hearers only, deceiving your ownselves. James 1:22

Word Enrichment

Doer - (poietes); A performer; one who performs from a script. Poietes/doer is one who reads a script and then acts out what the script says.

Many times we read the Word of God even hear it taught, however, we fail to do the Word of God. We must put the Word of God into action in our life. Just as a performer reads a script and acts out what the script says, this is what we must do with the Word. Act as if the Word of God is true. The children of Israel were told to do two things and they would see and experience the salvation of God in the midst of their circumstances.

They were told to (1) Stand still and (2) Fear Not! These are actions that we must do also. Believe the Word of God. Act on the Word of God. The Word says that you are free - so walk in the freedom Christ Jesus gave to you. Don't listen to the words of the enemy that are against the Word of God.

We cannot fulfill the word of God on our own. This is why God gave us His Holy Spirit. As the Holy Spirit leads and guides us into the truth of God's Word, we must walk in obedience.

What has God told you to do?
Have you done it? Has fear hindered you?
What are you going to do about it?

If God has told you to do something then God will supply the ability and the power for you to do it. You can be a doer of the word without fear because God is on your side!

Believe the Word of God. Act on the Word of God. God's Word says that you are free - so walk in the freedom Christ Jesus gave to you. Don't listen to the words of the enemy that are against the Word of God.

For I know the thoughts that I think toward you, saith the LORD, thoughts of peace, and not of evil, to give you an expected end Jeremiah 29: 11

We are called to be the doers of the Word of God. One of the primary ways the enemy hinders the work of the Lord in the earth is to get the believer to walk in fear. Fear will cause us to sabotage the plans and purpose of God in our life. When we are pursuing the purpose of God for our life, the enemy will fight us with fear. Trouble comes and the enemy tells us we cannot accomplish our goals. This won't work. We become afraid of failure.

We stop working on our goals. The enemy speaks to our minds to make us doubt if God really spoke to us. If we dwell on these thoughts, we will give up completely - we will not do what God has told us. This means we will walk in disobedience.

Don't allow fear of the enemy cause you to sabotage God's plans for your life. God has equipped you to fulfill what He has given you. As you stay focused on God's word to you, there will always be troubling situations however, continue to persevere in the midst of adversity. Don't lose focus on what you are to do. God is with you.

Be a doer of what God has given you to accomplish. Being confident of this very thing, that he which hath begun a good work in you will perform it until the day of Jesus Christ: Phil. 1:6

ACTIVE FAITH PRAYER:

O Lord, help me to walk in faith and remain focused on Your word to me that I may allow You to complete Your purpose in and through my life. In Jesus' name, Amen.

ACTIVE FAITH CONFESSION:

I am confident of this very thing, that he which hath begun a good work in me will perform it until the day of Jesus Christ.

Friday: Focus! Focus! Focus!
"TRUST GOD'S FAITHFULNESS"

This I recall to my mind, therefore have I hope. It is of the LORD'S mercies that we are not consumed, because his compassions fail not. 23 They are new every morning: great is thy faithfulness. Lamentations 3:21-23

Word Enrichment

Recall - (shuv); to tum oneself around; to tum to Jehovah; to restore; the basic meaning of shuv is movement back to the point of departure.

Mind - (lev); the heart, middle, or the center of something. Lev is used for the totality of man's inner immaterial nature. These are the deepest an innermost feelings. In the Bible, the entire spectrum of our human emotions is related to and attributed to the heart.

Hope - (yachal); to wait; to expect; to be patient. Yachal is rooted in God

Mercies - (chesed); unfailing love; favor; benevolence; good will; loyalty

Faithfulness - (emunah); firmness; steadiness; trust; honesty

As we read through the beginning of this chapter we see that Jeremiah was rehearsing all the bad things that had happened to him and God's people. Does that sound familiar. We often rehearse things that have gone wrong for us or the things that we have done that were wrong. We blame God, self, or others.

No matter what has happened God is not mad at you! God still loves you and has a wonderful plan for your life. He loves, forgives, saves, heals, and delivers every believer who calls on Him from every destruction.

At verse 21, we see Jeremiah coming to the truth that God is still with him. He had to shuv/recall to his mind. To *shuv* is *to return to the point of departure.* Jeremiah had departed from his belief that God is with him .

This departure caused him to review in his mind all the negatives of live. His hope was gone until he returned his thinking to the faithfulness of God, realizing he was still experiencing new mercies of God each day! Even in the midst of rough situations, God's compassions did not fail Jeremiah. God is on your side. His compassions will not fail you either!

Whatever has happened begin to trust God now as your Salvation, Healer, and Deliver from fears and torment. God is faithful!!!

What situation are you in that you cannot see God working on your behalf!

Write and Meditate on the Psalms 121 today.

_____
_____
_____
_____
_____
_____
_____
_____
_____
_____
_____
_____
_____
_____
_____
_____
_____
_____

ACTIVE FAITH PRAYER:

I look to You Lord for You are my help and my strength. Thank You for Your faithfulness to me. In Jesus' name, Amen.

ACTIVE FAITH CONFESSION:

I will lift up mine eyes unto the hills, from whence cometh my help. My help cometh from the LORD, which made heaven and earth.

Notes:

Week 3
Trust God's Presence
Isaiah 41:10

Fear thou not; for I am with thee: be not dismayed; for I am thy God."I will strengthen thee; yea, I will help thee; yea, I will uphold thee with the right hand of my righteousness.

Word Enrichment

Dismay (sha'a); bewildered; to gaze about looking for help; to look around in amazement

Dismay - to become afraid or discouraged and have a loss of confidence at the prospect of trouble or danger; to become afraid of trouble which one does no know how to resolve; to deprive of power

Strengthen (ames); to be alert physically or mentally with courage; fortify; to make strong

Help (azar); to surround, i.e. protect or aid

Uphold (tamak); sustain; to help; follow close; maintain

The word *fear* in this verse of scripture is *yare'*. The yare' that God is saying here is that we don't have to be afraid, timid, or anxious. If God says "Do not fear" it must be because there is something the enemy is bringing that in the natural would cause us to fear.
There are many situations that occur in life that the enemy seeks to use as an avenue to cause the believer to fear. No matter how or what the enemy comes against us with, God tells us to "Fear not!"
We can put our confidence in the Lord Jesus Christ who loved us so much He gave His life for us. The Bible tells us in Romans that even while we were yet sinners, Christ died for us. Christ died and arose from the dead with all power to give us power over the enemy.
God's abiding presence is always with the Christian. Fear Not! If you don't feel God's presence - PRAISE HIM! God dwells in the atmosphere of praise and worship.

If you do feel afraid because of pressures of life, grief, illness, sorrow of heart, divorce, etc., you can bring the presence of heaven right where you are by thanking God for His goodness and faithfulness. Psalms 22:3 lets us know that God dwells in the midst of praise! To dwell means to stay. God will stay right there with you. If you draw near to God, God will draw near to you.

Acknowledging God's presence provokes Him to let you feel His presence near - right in your spirit! Acknowledging God's presence will change your atmosphere. Fear cannot stay where faith in God is.

In this verse of scripture two exhortations are given: (I) Fear not and (2) Be not dismayed. When we become afraid and don't know what to do, we often look around for help. There are some situations that only God can help us through. Trust God's faithfulness to His Word to you.

We lose spiritual power, emotional power, and physical power when we negatively fear. When we are in the midst of troubling and perplexing situations we look around for help. As we see in the life of David through the Psalms, oftentimes there is no help other than God.

Monday: Trust God's Presence
"SUBMIT YOURSELF TO GOD"

Submit yourselves therefore to God. Resist the devil. and he will flee from you. James 4:7

Word Enrichment

Submit - to yield to; surrender; to obey; to defer to another's opinion or decision; to agree. The opposite of submit is to fight.

Submit - (hupotasso); to place in an orderly fashion under. Hupatasso is made up of two words: hupo, which means under. Hupo implies placement i.e., beneath, or to place under.

The other word is tasso. Tasso means to place, set in order or in its proper category. Tasso has inherent in its meaning order, categorization, and classification.

Resist - (anthistemi); to oppose; to act or make efforts in opposition to; to do something that prevents or inhibits some effect from taking place.

Flee - to run away from danger or from pursuers; to run from a place or person; to take flight.

We must agree with the Word of God and walk in obedience to it. This is how we place ourselves under the authority of God's Word. As we place our will and our words in order under God's Word, the rest of our life will begin to line up with the blessings that God has for us. Our life will begin to have more order as we place it under God's authority.

To overcome negative fears one must first submit to God and God's Word. Only after you have done that will you be able to resist the enemy. In submitting to God, you are resisting the enemy. Concentrate on submitting to God not on resisting the enemy. Resistance is a process.

For example, when you have a wooden deck put in your yard it must be treated with a weather resistant to prevent corrosion from the rain, now and inclement weather. As you continually submit to God with complete obedience, the Word of God in you will resist the enemy and prevent the corrosion of corrupt thinking to overtake your life.

Stand still! Remain firm in the Word by submitting your thoughts and conduct to God. You w ill see the enemy flee. The enemy will run away from us, not because of us, but because of Christ in us.

LOCATION - LOCATION – LOCATION

Romans 10:17 tells us, *So then faith cometh by hearing, and hearing by the word of God.* Hearing in this scripture means, *to understand; to hear with the ear of the mind; to hear effectually or so as to perform or grant what is spoken; to obey.*

God equates hearing with obedience. As we hear the Word of God over and over again, and walk in obedience, our faith will mature. We must know the Word to trust the Word. In scripture, to know is to have an intimate relationship with. How intimate is your relationship with the Word?

As we become intimate with the Word, our desire will be toward a healthy fear of the Lord. We will begin to trust God's presence. If we are distant from the Word of God, we will feel and believe that God is distant from us and this will bring fear and torment of the enemy. Put yourself in a location to hear and be taught the Word of God. Put your heart and mind in a position to submit to the Word of God.

Where are you in your obedience to the Word of God?

Can you be located or found in the place of submission to the Word or is it difficult to obey?

ACTIVE FAITH PRAYER:
Thank You God for Your presence with me. In Jesus' name, Amen.

ACTIVE FAITH CONFESSION:
I will submit my thoughts and conduct to the authority of God's Word. I will resist the thoughts and conduct of the enemy. I will hear the Word of God and obey it.

Notes:
_____
_____
_____
_____
_____
_____
_____
_____
_____
_____
_____
_____
_____
_____
_____
_____
_____
_____
_____
_____
_____
_____
_____

Tuesday: Trust God's Presence
"MEDITATE THE WORD"

This book of the law shall not depart out of thy mouth; but thou shalt meditate therein day and night. that thou mayest observe to do according to all that is written therein: for then thou shalt make thy way prosperous, and then thou shalt have good success. Joshua 1:8

Word Enrichment

Meditate - (hagah); to mutter to oneself, to whisper, to speak. It is possible that the Scriptures were read audibly during the process of meditation. Hagah also describes the low moaning sound of a dove.

Many people think that meditation is a difficult discipline. If you know how to worry, then you know how to meditate. Worry is simply negative meditation. In meditation, you review something over and over again either in your mind or aloud. Instead of reviewing a problem, rehearse in your mind the answer which is found in the Word of God.

Meditation allows us to quiet our spirit and soul from the things that daily clamor for our attention. We become quiet within. There is no frenzied and hurried activity during meditation! Simply, quietly, and plainly be in the presence of God knowing that God is with you. Meditating on a verse or passage of scripture allows us to marinate in the Word and gives the Word opportunity to saturate throughout our inner being. In meditation we marinate and saturate the Word!!!

Basics of meditating: Take five minutes. Sit, stand, or lie down in a relaxed position in a quiet place where you cannot be disturbed. Inhale deep breaths and count as you exhale. Counting your breath helps to practice the ability of thinking of one thing at a time. Simply breathe and count. If other thoughts come, realize you are straying from your instructions and gently bring yourself to counting again. Do this for three to five minutes twice a day. The third time you do this during the day, review a meditation scripture or just quietly give thanks to God.

You can also spend time in silence before Him. An important aspect of meditation is follow-through. Decide the time and place you will spend meditating, not the time you'd like to spend meditating. Growth and change take time. Be determined to stick with it. Be faithful. The benefits of meditating are tremendous. The more you dwell on the Word of God, the more it will season your soul and spirit. Be faithful. You will see and experience the benefits of meditation.

Write and Meditate Psalms 1 throughout the day:

ACTIVE FAITH PRAYER:
Thank You God for Your presence with me and for blessing me today. In Jesus name, Amen.

ACTIVE FAITH CONFESSION:
I shall be like a tree planted by the rivers of water, that brings forth his fruit in his season; My leaf also shall not wither; and whatsoever I do, it shall prosper.

Notes:

Wednesday: Trust God's Presence
"BELIEVE AND SPEAK THE WORD OF GOD"

That if thou shalt confess with thy mouth the Lord Jesus, and shalt believe in thine heart that God hath raised him from the dead, thou shalt be saved. 10 For with the heart man believeth unto righteousness; and with the mouth confession is made unto salvation. Romans 10:9-10

Word Enrichment

Confess - (homologeo); to say the same as; to speak the same with or consent to the desire of another; to covenant; to give thanks; To acknowedge; to speak in harmony with the truth.

Salvation - (soteria); deliverance; preservation; safety; Soteria is the spiritual and eternal salvation granted by God to those who believe on Jesus Christ.

Soteria is also used of material and temporal deliverance from danger suffering, sickness, etc.

We must begin to confess what the Word of God says. What have you been saying? Have you been speaking fear filled words of the enemy or have you been speaking the faith filled Word of God?

In Matthew 4 when Jesus was tempted of the devil, He who is the Word made flesh spoke the Word to the enemy. We must do the same. To be saved from the destruction and torments of fear, you must begin to believe and say what God has said to you and about you. Do not allow the enemy to pervert your thinking and your words any longer. Jesus tells us in John 6:63 that the words He speaks are spirit and life. We are also told in Proverbs 18:21 that death and life are in the power of the tongue. Words do something. Words create!
 We believe that Jesus came to give us life more abundantly and that Jesus speaks words that are spirit and life. SPEAK

WHAT JESUS SPEAKS!!! The Word of God will change your life, your circumstances and your situations.

Amos 3:3 asks 'Can two walk together, except they be agreed?' You cannot walk with God and receive all that God has for you until you walk in agreement with God's Word. If you don't agree with God you will agree with the enemy who is totally against you and perverts what God has said. God is always for your good.

If our confidence in God's word is weak, we will not have good spiritual vision. When this happens, we cannot boldly speak victory. Elisha could speak confidently and boldly because he saw clearly. His eyes were opened because his heart had received and believed the word of God.

The young man saw the danger, Elisha saw the protective hand of Almighty God in the midst of the danger. When our focus is rooted in the Sovereignty and power of Almighty God, we won't be easily disturbed and fear the troubles on earth.

BELIEVE AND AGREE WITH GOD!!!

~ What situation is causing my heart to be fearful? Anxious?
~Am I speaking faith or fear?

Today choose a situation in your life that has caused you to be fearful. Believe, speak, and spend time meditating Isaiah 41:10 aloud to yourself about this situation.

We must become disciplined in speaking life. Fear will dissipate as we believe and speak the Word of God which is the only life giving force! The Word of God can and will overcome any fearful situation that life brings to us.

ACTIVE FAITH PRAYER:

Thank You, Lord for Your presence with me. I am grateful that You are faithful to Your word that You will never leave me nor forsake me. Thank You for guiding me by Your word and Your Holy Spirit. In Jesus name, Amen.

ACTIVE FAITH CONFESSION:
I believe God. God is with me and is saving me from the torments of fear.

Notes:

Thursday: Trust God's Presence
"Be a Doer of the Word"

But be ye doers of the word, and not hearers only, deceiving your own selves. James 1:22

Word Enrichment

Doer - (poietes); A performer; one who performs from a script. Poietes/doer is one who reads a script and then acts out what the script says.

Many times we read the Word of God even hear it taught, however, we fail to do the Word of God. We must put the Word of God into action in our life. Just as a performer reads a script and acts out what the script says, this is what we must do with the Word. Act as if the Word of God is true.

The children of Israel were told to do two things and they would see and experience the salvation of God in the midst of their circumstances. They were told to (1) Stand still and (2) Fear Not! These are actions that we must do also.

Believe the Word of God. Act on the Word of God. The Word says that you are free - so walk in the freedom Christ Jesus gave to you. Don't listen to the words of the enemy that are against the Word of God.

We cannot fulfill the word of God on our own. This is why God gave us His Holy Spirit. As the Holy Spirit leads and guides us into the truth of God's Word, we must walk in obedience.

What has God told you to do?
Have you done it? Has fear hindered you?
What are you going to do about it?

If God has told you to do something then God will supply the ability and the power for you to do it. You can be a doer of the word without fear because God is on your side!

Isaiah 41:10 says "Fear not" and "Be not dismayed ... " Have you done this? What has caused you to fear? How can you overcome this? What has caused you to become dismayed? What can you do about this?

Notes:

_____
_____
_____
_____
_____
_____
_____
_____
_____
_____
_____
_____
_____
_____
_____
_____

ACTIVE FAITH PRAYER:
Lord, help me to hear, understand, and obey Your word to me. Let me be a doer of Your word, O God. In Jesus' name, Amen.

ACTIVE FAITH CONFESSION:
I will walk in faith and be a doer of God's word.

Friday: Trust God's Presence
"TRUST GOD'S FAITHFULNESS"

This I recall to my mind, therefore have I hope. 22 It is of the LORD'S mercies that we are not consumed, because his compassions fail not. 23 They are new every morning: great is thy faithfulness. Lamentations 3:21-23

Word Enrichment

Recall- (shuv); to turn oneself around; to turn to Jehovah; to restore; the basic meaning of shuv is movement back to the point of departure.

Mind - (lev); the heart, middle, or the center of something. Lev is used for the totality of man's inner immaterial nature. These are the deepest and innermost feelings. In the Bible, the entire spectrum of our human emotions is related to and attributed to the heart.

Hope - (yachal); to wait; to expect; to be patient. Yachal is rooted in God

Mercies - (chesed); unfailing love; favor; benevolence; good will; loyalty

Faithfulness - (emunah); firmness; steadiness; trust; honesty

As we read through the beginning of this chapter we see that Jeremiah was rehearsing all the bad things that had happened to him and God's people. Does that sound familiar. We often rehearse things that have gone wrong for us or the things that we have done that were wrong. We blame God, self, or others.

No matter what has happened God is not mad at you! God still loves you and has a wonderful plan for your life. He loves, forgives, saves, heals, and delivers every believer who calls on Him from every destruction. At verse 21, we see Jeremiah coming to the truth that God is still with him. He had to shuv/recall to his mind. To shuv is to return to the point of departure. Jeremiah had departed from his belief that God is with him.

This departure caused him to review in his mind all the negatives of live. His hope was gone until he returned his thinking to the faithfulness of God, realizing he was still experiencing new mercies of God each day! Even in the midst of rough situations, God's compassions did not fail Jeremiah. God is on your side.

Whatever has happened begin to trust God now as your Salvation, Healer, and Deliverer from fears and torment. God is faithful! In our opening text, God was leading His children along. They were fine until they saw the enemy! After they saw the enemy the children of Israel began to fear which was followed by murmuring and complaining to Moses.

God did not beat them over the head! He gently told them, "Fear not, stand still, and see My salvation." This is what we must remember to do when adverse situations come our way. Don't look at and meditate all the negatives: what has gone wrong and what doesn't look right. Recall to your mind the goodness and mercies of the Lord. This gives stability and hope.

~ What situation are you in that you cannot see God working on your behalf?

God is so committed to us that God has named His only Son Immanuel which means "God with us." The names of God reveal the nature and faithfulness of God's presence with His people.

Meditate on the following names of God today:

Jehovah Jireh - God is my Provider. Genesis 22:8-14
Jehovah Rohi - The Lord is my Shepherd. Psalms 23: 1
Jehovah Shalom - the Lord is my Peace. Judges 6:24

Write and Meditate   Lamentations 3:21-23

_____
_____
_____
_____

ACTIVE FAITH PRAYER:
Thank You God for the faithfulness of Your presence with me, in Jesus' name, Amen.

ACTIVE FAITH CONFESSION:
This I recall to my mind, therefore have hope. It is of the LORD mercies that we are not consumed, because his compassions fail no They are new every morning: great is thy faithfulness. Thank You Jesus!

Week 4
God Will Save!
Isaiah 35:4

Say to them *that are* of a fearful heart, Be strong, fear not: behold, your God will come *with* vengeance, *even* God *with* a recompence; he will come and save you.

Word Enrichment

Fearful (mahar); to hurry; to cause to make in a haste; rash; swift

Strong (hazaq); courageous; be attached; to conquer. This word hazaq was frequently used to describe battle scenes.

Save (Yasha); to be delivered; saved; to get help; give victory. It is noteworthy that the personal name of the Lord, Jesus, is derived from this root word Yasha.

Isaiah is proclaiming a message of hope to strengthen and comfort the people of God. Many people have been afraid, wounded, and weakened by various situations in life. We may have at times even suffered a seemingly defeat. Defeat is not failure until you quit.

Don't throw in the towel. When we start believing that defeat is failure we will begin to have a fearful heart. God is able to save us from those things the enemy would use against us to destroy us.

Say to those who are of a fearful heart "*Be strong.* "A fearful heart is a heart that has been weakened and has become afraid. When gripped by an unexpected situation, fear can cause us to react hastily. The wrong things can be said out of fear. The wrong things can be done quickly out of a fearful heart. Quite often, the things that are done hastily out of a fearful heart are things that will be regretted.

When we act out of a fearful heart we won't take time to think or pray. There will be situations that occur in life that will take us by surprise. This is why we must seek to daily be in fellowship with God. God has the answer for every situation that can cause us to fear.

Sometimes we are afraid to love because our love has been abused or taken advantage of. When this happens we become guarded. Love makes us vulnerable. When we are hurt we do not want to be vulnerable again so we become afraid to open our heart to love again. The enemy will use this fear to destroy us.

We are created in the image of God, therefore, it is our nature to love and be loved. We fear loving again because we do not want to be hurt again. When we've been hurt we must trust God to heal the broken and wounded places in our heart and bring wholeness to our being. God does not want us to be destroyed by unforgiveness, bitterness, or anger that can arise within us when we've been wounded.

God is not only concerned about the salvation of our soul; He is also concerned about our economic situation, our emotional well being and our spiritual growth. God desires to save us from anything that would bring harm to us, especially negative and hurting emotions.

Notes:

ACTIVE FAITH PRAYER:

Lord, help me walk with You, not ahead of You in haste, nor behind You in fear. Let me walk with You in confidence that You will save me. In Jesus name, Amen.

ACTIVE FAITH CONFESSION:

I will be courageous in the Lord. My heart trusts in God. God will come and save me.

Monday: God Will Save
"SUBMIT YOURSELF TO GOD"

Submit yourselves therefore to God. Resist the devil, and he will flee from you. James 4:7

Word Enrichment

Submit - to yield to; surrender; to obey; to defer to another's opinion or decision; to agree. The opposite of submit is to fight.

Submit - (hupotasso); to place in an orderly fashion under. Hupa tasso is made up of two words: hupo, which means under. Hupo implies placement i.e., beneath, or to place under.

The other word is tasso. Tasso means to place, set in order or in its proper category. Tasso has inherent in its meaning order, categoriza tion, and classification.

Resist - (anthistemi); to oppose; to act or make efforts in opposition to; to do something that prevents or inhibits some effect from taking place.

Flee - to run away from danger or from pursuers; to run from a place or person; to take flight.

    We must agree with the Word of God and walk in obedience to it. This is how we place ourselves under the authority of God's Word. As we place our will and our words in order under God's Word, the rest of our life will begin to line up with the blessings that God has for us. Our life will begin to have more order as we place it under God's authority.
    To overcome negative fears one must first submit to God and God's Word. Only after you have done that will you be able to resist the enemy.

In submitting to God, you are resisting the enemy. Concentrate on submitting to God not on resisting the enemy. Resistance is a process. For example, when you have a wooden deck put in your yard it must be treated with a weather resistant to prevent corrosion from the rain, snow and inclement weather. As you continually submit to God with complete obedience, the Word of God in you will resist the enemy and prevent the corrosion of corrupt thinking to overtake your life.

Stand still! Remain firm in the Word by submitting your thoughts and conduct to God. You will see the enemy flee. The enemy will run away from us, not because of us, but because of Christ in us.

Those that came to Jesus in the midst of fearful and devastating life situations were saved when they submitted to the word of the Lord.

Read Mark 5:2-34

We find that this woman had an issue! An issue is an outgoing, an outflow. She had an issue of blood. It was a life paralyzing, life threatening situation which she had to deal with for twelve long years. She found no help or healing from the many physicians. She went to them with a mindset to be submitted to their diagnosis and their prescriptions. She was dismayed which caused her to continue looking around for help. Finally she was healed by Jesus. How can this be? Jesus did not say a word to this woman until after power had left Him and surged through her body and down to her issue.

She was willing to submit to He who is the Word. She knew the Word had been healing people of all kinds of diseases. She confessed over and over *"If I can touch the hem of His garment I shall be made whole."* She kept pressing through the crowd even though she should not have been in the crowd. By law she was an unclean woman. Faith without works is dead. She had to do something. She submitted to the Word by faith and she was healed. Jesus said her faith healed her of that plague! Issues plague us. Issues cripple us.

We look around for help. Be determined to submit to the Word of God and put feet to your faith.

ACTIVE FAITH PRAYER:

Lord, each issue that is causing me to have a fearful heart, I bring it to You. I touch Your word with my faith believing that I shall be made whole. In Jesus name, Amen.

ACTIVE FAITH CONFESSION:
God is healing the hurting and wounded places in my life.

Notes:

Tuesday: God Will Save
"MEDITATE THE WORD"

This book of the law shall not depart out of thy mouth; but thou shalt meditate therein day and night. that thou mayest observe to do according to all that is written therein: for then thou shalt make thy way prosperous, and then thou shalt have good success. Joshua 1:8

Word Enrichment

Meditate - (hagah); to mutter to oneself, to whisper, to speak. It is possible that the Scriptures were read audibly during the process of meditation. Hagah also describes the low moaning sound of a dove.

Many people think that meditation is a difficult discipline. If you know how to worry, then you know how to meditate. Worry is simply negative meditation. In meditation, you review something over and over again either in your mind or aloud. Instead of reviewing a problem, rehearse in your mind the answer which is found in the Word of God.

Meditation allows us to quiet our spirit and soul from the things that daily clamor for our attention. We become quiet within. There is no frenzied and hurried activity during meditation! Simply, quietly, and plainly be in the presence of God knowing that God is with you. Meditating on a verse or passage of scripture allows us to marinate in the Word and gives the Word opportunity to saturate throughout our inner being. In meditation we marinate and saturate the Word!!!

Basics of meditating: Take five minutes. Sit, stand, or lie down in a relaxed position in a quiet place where you cannot be disturbed. Inhale deep breaths and count as you exhale. Counting your breath helps to practice the ability of thinking of one thing at a time. Simply breathe and count. If other thoughts come, realize you are straying from your instructions and gently bring yourself to counting again. Do this for three to five minutes twice a day.

The third time you do this during the day, review a meditation scripture or just quietly give thanks to God.

You can also spend time in silence before Him. An important aspect of meditation is follow-through. Decide the time and place you will spend meditating, not the time you'd like to spend meditating. Growth and change take time. Be determined to stick with it. Be faithful. The benefits of meditating are tremendous. The more you dwell on the Word of God, the more it will season your soul and spirit. Be faithful. You will see and experience the benefits of meditation.

Write and Meditate Psalms 27 throughout the day:

Be determined to stick with it. Be faithful. The benefits of meditating are tremendous. The more you dwell on the Word of God, the more it will season your soul and spirit. Be faithful. You will see and experience the benefits of meditation.

ACTIVE FAITH PRAYER:

Shew me thy ways, O LORD; teach me thy paths. Lead me in thy truth, and teach me: for thou art the God of my salvation; on thee do I wait all the day. In Jesus name, Amen.

ACTIVE FAITH CONFESSION:
I will believe to see the goodness of the Lord in the land of the living. I will be of good courage and He shall strengthen my heart.

Notes:

Wednesday: God Will Save
"BELIEVE AND SPEAK THE WORD OF GOD"

That if thou shalt confess with thy mouth the Lord Jesus, and shalt believe in thine heart that God hath raised him from the dead, thou shalt be saved. 10 For with the heart man believeth unto righteousness; and with the mouth confession is made unto salvation. Romans 10:9-10

Word Enrichment

Confess - (homologeo); to say the same as; to speak the same with or consent to the desire of another; to covenant; to give thanks; acknowledge; speak in harmony with the truth.

Salvation - (soteria); deliverance; preservation; safety; Soteria is the spiritual and eternal salvation granted by God to those who believe in Jesus Christ. Soteria is also used of material and temporal deliverance from danger, suffering, sickness, etc.

We must begin to confess what the Word of God says. What have you been saying? Have you been speaking fear filled words of the enemy or have you been speaking the faith filled Word of God? In Matthew 4 when Jesus was tempted of the devil, He who is the Word made flesh spoke the Word to the enemy. We must do the same.

To be saved from the destruction and torments of fear, you must begin to believe and say what God has said to you and about you. Do not allow the enemy to pervert your thinking and your words any longer. Jesus tells us in John 6:63 that the words He speaks are Spirit and life. We are also told in Proverbs 18:21 that death and life are in the power of the tongue. Words do something. Words create! We believe that Jesus came to give us life more abundantly and that Jesus speaks words that are spirit and life. SPEAK WHAT JESUS SPEAKS!!! The Word of God will change your life, your circumstances and your situations.

Amos 3:3 asks 'Can two walk together, except they be agreed?' You cannot walk with God and receive all that God has for you until you walk in agreement with God's Word. If you don't agree with God you will agree with the enemy who is totally against you and perverts what God has said. God is always for your good.

BELIEVE AND AGREE WITH GOD!!!

What has caused my heart to be fearful? Anxious?
~ What am I saying about it?
~Am I speaking faith or fear?

Today choose a situation in your life that has caused you to be fearful. Believe, speak, and spend time meditating Isaiah 41:10 aloud to yourself about this situation.

Notes:
_____
_____
_____
_____
_____
_____
_____
_____
_____
_____
_____
_____
_____
_____
_____
_____
_____
_____
_____

ACTIVE FAITH PRAYER:
Thank You Lord for being my Savior, Healer, and Deliverer from all fear and torment. Let me be transformed by the renewing of my mind by Your Word. In Jesus name, Amen.

ACTIVE FAITH CONFESSION:
Behold, God is my salvation; I will trust, and not be afraid: for the LORD JEHOVAH is my strength and my song; he also is become my salvation.

Thursday: God Will Save
"BE A DOER OF THE WORD"

But be ye doers of the word, and not hearers only, deceiving your ownselves. James 1:22

Word Enrichment

Doer - (poietes); A performer; one who performs from a script. Poietes/doer is one who reads a script and then acts out what the script says.

Many times we read the Word of God even hear it taught, however, we fail to do the Word of God. We must put the Word of God into action in our life. Just as a performer reads a script and acts out what the script says, this is what we must do with the Word. Act as if the Word of God is true. The children of Israel were told to do two things and they would see and experience the salvation of God in the midst of their circumstances. They were told to (1) Stand still and (2) Fear Not! These are actions that we must do also.

Believe the Word of God. Act on the Word of God. The Word says that you are free - so walk in the freedom Christ Jesus gave to you. Don't listen to the words of the enemy that are against the Word of God. We cannot fulfill the word of God on our own. This is why God gave us His Holy Spirit. As the Holy Spirit leads and guides us into the truth of God's Word, we must walk in obedience.

What has God told you to do?
Have you done it? Has fear hindered you?
What are you going to do about it?

If God has told you to do something then God will supply the ability and the power for you to do it. You can be a doer of the word without fear because God is on your side!

Read Mark 5:21-43

In the midst of coming to Jesus, falling at the Master's feet, and asking Jesus to came and heal his daughter, Jesus' attention was diverted to a woman with another issue - an issue of blood. While Jesus dealt with this issue, Jairus' daughter died. Jesus heard and told Jairus to do two things: (1) Don't be afraid, and (2) Only believe. There had to have been some belief in the healing power of Jesus for Jairus to even come to Him. Fear would have taken this away. That's why Jesus had to deal with it immediately.

This was a *rhema* word to Jairus. Rhema is *God's specific word for a specific situation.* This is the word that God puts in your spirit and you know that you know you know God said it. You don't even know how you know - it is just in your spirit by God's Spirit!!! No person and no situation can take a rhema word from you.

Jairus trusted in and obeyed his rhema word from the Lord Jesus. Had he become afraid and not believed Jesus, Jairus probably would have trusted in the "other" word that said his daughter was dead. He would have left Jesus there and went home to bury his daughter. Jairus was a doer of the word of the Lord to him. He took Jesus to his home and Jesus raised his daughter.

When faced with alarming situations that life presents, turn to the Lord for His word to you in the midst of whatever you are facing.

Notes:
_____
_____
_____
_____
_____
_____
_____

ACTIVE FAITH PRAYER:

Lord, teach me to hear and know Your voice and Your rhema word to me so that I can be a doer of Your word and not a hearer only. In Jesus' name, Amen.

ACTIVE FAITH CONFESSION:

I am a doer of God's word. I will walk in obedience to the Word of God. I will not fear. God will save me.

Friday: God Will Save
'TRUST GOD'S FAITHFULNESS"

This I recall to my mind, therefore have I hope. 22 It is of the LORD'S mercies that we are not consumed, because his compassions fail not. 23 They are new every morning: great is thy faithfulness. Lamentations 3:21-23

Word Enrichment

Recall- (shuv); to turn oneself around; to turn to Jehovah; to restore; the basic meaning of shuv is movement back to the point of departure.

Mind - (lev); the heart, middle, or the center of something. Lev is used for the totality of man's inner immaterial nature. These are the deepest and innermost feelings. In the Bible, the entire spectrum of our human emotions is related to and attributed to the heart.

Hope - (yachal); to wait; to expect; to be patient. Yachal is rooted in God

Mercies - (chesed); unfailing love; favor; benevolence; good will; loyalty

Faithfulness - (emunah); firmness; steadiness; trust; honesty

As we read through the beginning of this chapter we see that Jeremiah was rehearsing all the bad things that had happened to him and God's people. Does that sound familiar. We often rehearse things that have gone wrong for us or the things that we have done that were wrong. We blame God, self, or others.

No matter what has happened God is not mad at you! God still loves you and has a wonderful plan for your life. He loves, forgives, saves, heals, and delivers every believer who calls on Him from every destruction. At verse 21, we see Jeremiah coming to the truth that God is still with him. He had to shuv/recall to his mind. To shuv is to return to the point of departure. Jeremiah had departed from his belief that God is with him.

This departure caused him to review in his mind all the negatives of live. His hope was gone until he returned his thinking to the faithfulness of God, realizing he was still experiencing new mercies of God each day! Even in the midst of rough situations, God's compassions did not fail Jeremiah. God is on your side.

Whatever has happened begin to trust God now as your Salvation, Healer, and Deliverer from fears and torment. God is faithful!!!

~ What situation are you in that you cannot see God working on your behalf?

Write and Meditate Psalms 69:30 today:

Notes:
_____
_____
_____
_____
_____
_____
_____
_____
_____
_____
_____

Word Enrichment

Praise (halal); to celebrate; glorify

Thanksgiving (todah); an extension of the hands; a confession. An offering of praise to God. Todah has its source in yadah.

Yadah - to speak out; confess; give thanks. The expression of thanks to God by way of praising.

Praise leads to thanksgiving. We surrender our hearts when we lift up our hands to the Lord in praise and adoration. Praise the Lord for his compassion to heal and deliver from fear and torment all those that come to Him in faith.

Notes:

ACTIVE FAITH PRAYER:

Thank You God for saving, loving, and caring for me. You have begun a great work in me and You will complete it. I praise You for being true to Your word and for being God. In Jesus name, Amen.

ACTIVE FAITH CONFESSION:

I will praise the name of God with a song, and will magnify him with thanksgiving.

Other Books by Patty Harris

Blessed are They that Mourn
Bible- Find - A - Word Puzzles (Vols. I-VII)
Comforting Those who Grieve
Conquering Holiday Grief
Fear Nots for Everyday
Fear Nots for Those who Grieve
God Has An APP for That!
Pray-er Points to Ponder
PrayerWalking!
Praying in the Key of "C"
Restoring the Gates of Prayer
Surviving the Death of a Loved One
The T.A.S.K.S. of the Pray-er
The Truth about Strongholds
What You Can't Lose in the Midst of Loss

www.ingramcontent.com/pod-product-compliance
Lightning Source LLC
Chambersburg PA
CBHW020017050426
42450CB00005B/517